# A DAY IN THE LIFE
# Birds

### WHAT DO FLAMINGOS, OWLS, AND PENGUINS GET UP TO ALL DAY?

NEON SQUID

# Contents

# Welcome to the world of birds!

Birds are some of the world's most visible animals—I bet there's one outside your window right now! I fell in love with birds when I was very young, and that blossomed into a love of nature, islands, the oceans, and much more. Now I am the **principal curator of birds** at the Natural History Museum, in London, England, where I look after one of the largest bird collections in the world. I also do research on bird conservation in the United Kingdom, Australia, and Canada, and on remote islands in each and every ocean.

Join me as we embark on a journey to explore the huge diversity of birds across the world. We'll be looking at songs, nests, eggs, feeding, flying, behavior, and more. Each page shows something **interesting, exciting, or weird** about these wonderful creatures at a different time of the day—from the early morning dawn chorus to owls hunting at dusk.

Birds are **fascinating animals,** and there is so much to learn about them. How do they build safe and cozy nests? Why do they sing in the morning? How do they hunt for prey and escape from predators? I will explore these questions and answer many more. Let's have a look at a day in the life of birds!

### Dr. Alex Bond

## European robin

Both female and male robins sing, and they are among the first to start each morning. *Tick-ick-ick-ick!* This is a common sound across Europe.

# The dawn chorus

As the day begins and the sun is still below the horizon, a most remarkable noise rises up from forests, fields, and towns—the dawn chorus! All sorts of birds chirp, tweet, and warble to check in with their neighbors and let everyone know which patch is theirs.

## Varied thrush

In western North America, the varied thrush starts early and trills from the top of evergreen trees. It will move locations every 10–15 minutes to make sure its mate hears it.

**House lights and streetlights can confuse birds, making them sing at night.**

## Mangrove pitta

In South East Asia, mangrove pittas call out with a loud, sharp, short *hwa-hwa* or *wieuw-wieuw* every four seconds—usually from the tops of mangrove trees.

Some birds have changed their songs as human noises, such as cars on roads, have interfered with them.

## Tasmanian thornbill

The calls of Tasmanian thornbills start with *tsit-tsit, chee-cheeee-chee* and end with a bubbly *wit-wit-wit*, with trills and warbles in the middle. These calls strengthen the social bonds between mates and neighbors.

## Scissor-tailed flycatcher

Scissor-tailed flycatchers repeatedly give a short *whit* as they fly high, often pairing it with a soaring display. Then they appear to stop before letting out the final call, as if to tell predators, "I see you."

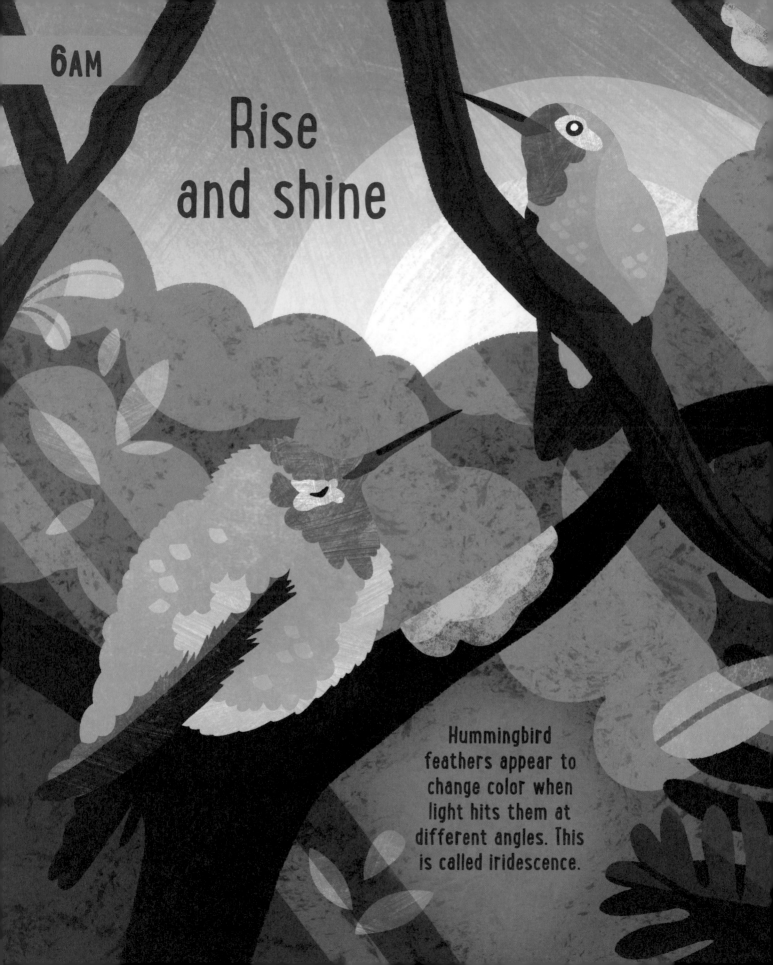

# Rise and shine

Hummingbird feathers appear to change color when light hits them at different angles. This is called iridescence.

As dawn breaks in the forests of South America, the air comes alive with the sounds of many birds starting their day. Perched on a branch, a broad-billed hummingbird slowly emerges from a **very deep sleep**.

When hummingbirds are awake, they use their energy quickly. So they need to feed on the **nectar of flowers**, such as honeysuckle or agave, almost constantly. Since the flowers are closed at night, the birds can't get a late-night snack if they feel a little hungry. To save energy each bird slows its heart rate, drops its body temperature, and enters a deep slumber. This is called torpor.

After the hummingbird warms up its core body temperature to 104°F (40°C) and fluffs up its feathers, it can head out for the day. It will visit flowers until it's time to go to bed!

**Meanwhile...** Out on the windy sea cliffs of the North Pacific, tufted puffins come out of their underground burrows to start the day. With a fresh breeze ruffling their straw-colored head plumes, they head out to sea in search of fish.

# Bower building

Only a little bit of sunshine reaches the floor of the rainforests of southern New Guinea, just north of Australia. But among the subtle green leaves there's a flash of bright red and yellow. It's a male flame bowerbird!

It's just before the **breeding season** and he wants to impress a female the best way he knows how—by building the perfect bower. A bower isn't exactly a nest, though it can look like one. It's a stage where the male will perform a **unique and elaborate ritual** while a female looks on. She will then decide whether or not to approach him.

The shape, size, placement, and colors of the bower must be just right, or else a female won't give the male the time of day. The flame bowerbird particularly likes blue items, like berries, that will stand out against the leaves. Building a bower is a tricky task, but it sure makes for a fancy first date!

Step one: Gather dried twigs and a few brown leaves.

Step two: Collect colorful berries.

Step three: Build
the bower and
wait for a female
to appear.

Gentoo penguins can go 330 ft (100 m) underwater on a single breath. That's more than the height of a 20-story building!

# Pebble thieves

On a cold, windy beach on the Antarctic Peninsula, gentoo penguins have started to build their nests. They may not look like much to you or me—just a pile of stones on the ground—but for these penguins, the pebbles that hold their eggs are **very precious**. Courting penguins even give each other pebbles as a way of showing their affection.

A female gentoo penguin is sitting on a completed nest, peacefully keeping her eggs warm. But **WATCH OUT!** Sometimes a particularly nice pebble can cause trouble when another penguin tries to steal it for their own nest. The thief needs to be careful though—if they're too slow, they run the risk of getting a sharp nibbling from the original owner's beak. Ouch!

# The dance of the flamingos

As the morning sun gets higher, birds start to get more active. High up in the Andes, a mountain range in South America, Andean flamingos (the largest and rarest flamingo) gather in salt lakes. Here, they form **giant flocks** that parade back and forth through the shallows. Like the bowerbirds and the penguins, they are strengthening the pair-bonds between mates.

Sticking together in a parade also ensures that all the flamingos **breed at the same time**. This is very important because all of the chicks will be looked after together. Parades can have as few as ten or as many as 100 birds.

When a flamingo swishes its curved bill through the water, it acts like a sieve to catch prey. The pink color of Andean flamingo feathers comes from the small, pink crustaceans they feed on. It's very much a case of "you are what you eat!"

# Nests and eggs

Every species of bird lays eggs. Some birds build nests to hold their eggs, while others don't. Some look after their chicks for months and months, and some lay the eggs and fly away. Inside the eggs, chicks develop until they are ready to hatch and come into the world.

### Maleo

The maleo doesn't sit on its eggs—it buries them in sand, like some sea turtles do. But rather than each pair having its own nest, they'll bury their eggs together with those from other maleos.

### Baya weaver

Some birds, like the baya weaver in South East Asia, build elaborate nests designed to keep predators out. This bird weaves a nest from reeds and grass that's suspended from a branch high up in the air—so predators can't reach it!

## Common eider

One of the coziest nests is probably that of the common eider, a type of sea duck. The female plucks soft downy feathers from her belly to line the nest. Once the eggs are laid, she'll sit, uninterrupted, for three to four weeks incubating the eggs (keeping them warm).

## Southern brown kiwi

Some birds lay a few small eggs. The kiwi does the opposite—it lays one giant egg!

The egg inside a kiwi

## Guillemot

Guillemots lay colorful eggs—from white to green and blue—with spots, flecks, and streaks. Because they lay their eggs on cliffs without nests and right next to their neighbors, scientists think the different colors help them identify their own eggs.

Swallows use the lower part of their beaks like a trowel to pick up mud.

They make up to 1,000 trips to collect mud for their nests!

# Eggs in the nest

It's been a tough few months for a pair of swallows. They spent the winter in Africa, before flying north to Europe for the summer. Once they arrived, they turned their attention to a very important task: building a nest where they would raise this year's chicks! They found a nice spot in the eaves of a barn and got to work.

The nests are made from **mud and spit (ew!)** and lined with grass stems and feathers, which the adult birds carried back in their tiny beaks and laid down in rows.

It took both parents two weeks to build the nest together. As days went by and the mud dried, the nest got harder and harder, becoming the perfect place to lay eggs and **raise this year's family**.

The female swallow is now sitting patiently on the eggs, keeping them warm. Incubating the eggs makes sure that the chicks are fully developed before they hatch. She's been doing this for 15 days, so the eggs could hatch at any moment now....

# Keeping eggs warm

An ostrich egg weighs more
than 250 chicken eggs!

To make sure the eggs are evenly warm, the male ostrich sticks his head in the nest to rotate them.

Keeping eggs at just the right temperature is very important. In many areas, this means incubating them to make sure they stay warm, but for a male common ostrich in Africa this also means **keeping them cool** and out of the hot midday sun.

Male ostriches, like this one, are in charge of the eggs and often incubate more than 30 every year. About a third of those are from the male's main partner, and the rest come from several other females that he's mated with. His **big fluffy feathers** keep the eggs at just the right temperature.

Ostrich eggs are the biggest bird eggs in the world, but that's not really surprising— ostriches can be more than 6½ ft (2 m) tall!

**Meanwhile...** Back in New Guinea, the flame bowerbird shows off his best dance moves, spreading his wings and presenting the berries. A female looks through the bower and is clearly impressed!

# Imposter in the nest

Deep in a European reedbed lies a nest. But something isn't quite right... While most birds lay their eggs in a nest and incubate them, some lay their eggs in the nests of other species and leave the nest's owners to raise their chicks. Talk about lazy parenting! A few weeks ago a **common cuckoo** laid her eggs in a reed warbler's nest. Common cuckoo eggs are larger than reed warbler eggs, and some reed warblers know something is up and can remove the imposter eggs from the nest before they hatch. But this reed warbler was fooled!

Then things got even worse. The cuckoo chick was the first to hatch—looking kind of like a naked chicken—and then it pushed all of the reed warbler eggs out of the nest! Amazingly, the warbler parents have continued to feed the intruder, even though it's now huge and **looks very different**. The cuckoo chick will soon develop wing feathers and be on its way, and the reed warblers will be none the wiser.

Birds laying their eggs in the nests of other species is called brood parasitism.

# The special chicks

It's lunchtime in the tundra of Siberia, a region in the north of Russia. There's a bustle of activity as two spoon-billed sandpipers watch over their newly hatched chicks. Most birds look after their own young and, for most species, the chicks need to be taken care of once they hatch. The parents keep them away from predators, teach them how to feed, and protect them from the elements of the outside world. This job is particularly important for these spoon-billed sandpipers—they're some of the **rarest birds** in the world!

There are only about 250–620 spoon-billed sandpipers on the planet, and they are critically endangered. Over the years, scientists have found only a few nests. These birds lay four eggs at a time, and the chicks leave the nest after about three weeks.

These chicks are a few weeks old and they're very hungry, so their parents take them to the shoreline for a healthy lunch. They feed on small animals in the mud using their oddly shaped bills. Some of the birds here have **leg tags**. This is so scientists can record their movements, survival, and breeding. If you see a bird with a leg band or tag, be sure to let a scientist know!

## The peregrine falcon

The fastest birds in the world, peregrine falcons are speed demons. They have pointed wings like jet fighters and can dive at speeds of up to 200 mph (320 kph)! Being this quick gives them the upper hand when hunting prey.

# Flight

Most birds can fly, but how they do that, and how fast or slow they go, depends on the shape and size of their wings. Discover what makes some bird species unique when it comes to taking flight.

## Easy glider

The bird with the largest wings in the world is the southern royal albatross—they are 11 ft (3.5 m) long! They can lock their wings open at the shoulder and soar for hours like gliders.

## Hummingbirds

To keep themselves in the air, hummingbirds beat their wings in a figure-eight motion, which means they have to flap them very quickly. From afar it may look like they are floating, but an Anna's hummingbird's wings actually flap around 80 times per second.

Some birds that live on islands have lost the ability to fly because they don't need to escape from predators.

## Wonderful wings

Not all birds use their wings just for flying—some use them to attract other birds. The pennant-winged nightjar and the standard-winged nightjar have long streamers to impress potential mates.

# A long flight

Bar-headed geese honk
loudly when migrating to keep
their flock together. They have
been heard from the summit
of Makalu, the fifth tallest
mountain in the world!

After breeding, many birds migrate so they can follow the warm temperatures and the food. Some migrations are hard, like the journey bar-headed geese undergo to **fly over the Himalayas**, the highest mountains in the world.

After breeding in the wetlands of Mongolia, China, and Pakistan, the geese take off for the winter. They fly in a **V-formation**, which helps them conserve energy. The geese are heading for the swamps, lakes, and rivers of India, Bangladesh, and Myanmar.

Flapping their wings, they rise to an altitude of 28,000 ft (8,500 m) to get over the tall peaks in a single flight. The air is very thin up here, but the geese have super-efficient breathing systems that help them cope with the lack of oxygen. They'll fly back in the spring along a similar route!

**Meanwhile...** The barn swallow chicks have hatched! Their parents will need to feed them flying insects for the next three weeks so they can grow.

# Soaring high, swooping low

As the afternoon sun warms the ground, hot air rises up in columns called thermals. Soaring up high is a majestic bald eagle. This North American bird of prey uses its long wings to **fly effortlessly** as it's pushed up by the rising air. It can adjust its direction with just a slight twitch of the "fingers" at the end of its wings. These are actually feathers that help the eagle make tiny course corrections without spending too much energy.

As our bald eagle makes its way over rivers and lakes, it looks down in search of something tasty to eat. Spotting a large salmon just under the surface, it circles down and hovers just above the water. Then, **SPLASH!** It strikes with its large hooked claws, or talons. It whips the fish out of the water and heads off to find somewhere peaceful to eat it.

Bald eagles cover a huge area when hunting. This is important because they need to eat the equivalent of 13 adult salmon each day to get the energy they need.

# Hungry penguins

Krill are a type of small crustacean.

Back in Antarctica, the first of the gentoo penguin chicks have hatched. They need feeding for the next three months until they're big enough to hunt on their own. The adults head out to sea, diving as far as 165 ft (50 m) below the water to catch krill or fish. They **store prey in their throats**. When they get back to the colony, they regurgitate the food to feed the waiting chicks. Tasty!

Penguin flippers are modified wings full of tiny, tightly packed feathers.

For the first three to four weeks after a chick is born, the parents have to coordinate their journeys very carefully so the chick isn't left alone for too long. They also need to make sure that the chick gets enough food so it can grow quickly.

After four weeks, the chicks in the colony will form large groups called crèches, and the adults will look after them as a group. This helps **protect the chicks** from predators. It also gives the adults a little bit of time off from parenting duty to look after themselves!

33

## Galápagos finches

On the Galápagos Islands, off the coast of South America, finches have evolved (adapted over time) to feed in different environmental conditions. You can tell what type of food each finch likes to eat by looking at the shape of its bill.

**Cocos finch**
Eats mainly insects

**Large ground finch**
Eats large seeds and fruit

**Vegetarian finch**
Eats leaves, fruit, and buds

**Common cactus finch**
Feeds on cactus pulp, fruit, and flowers

# Dinnertime

Like all living things, birds love a tasty meal. But how they eat depends on their bill, their tongue, where they live, and how they capture food. Getting a good meal is essential because birds need to feed not only themselves, but also their chicks!

## Scavengers

Bearded vultures are scavengers, meaning they eat things that are already dead—mostly large mammals. Their stomachs are very acidic, which helps them digest bones. Their hooked beaks help them pick apart tasty mouthfuls.

## Diving for food

In the oceans, birds like guillemots and penguins dive for fish, squid, and crustaceans. King penguins can dive more than 650 ft (200 m) because their wings are adapted for "flying" underwater!

## Pecking for dinner

Getting a meal is tricky for pileated woodpeckers. They use their chisel-like bills to make holes in trees so they can reach grubs and invertebrates such as ants and termites. Their long, sticky tongues help them capture and retrieve food.

**Woodpeckers have stiff tail feathers that they use to balance against tree trunks when feeding.**

## Hummingbird bills

How do hummingbirds get the sweet liquid deep inside flowers? Different species have evolved different bill shapes depending on which flowers they prefer! Curved for curved flowers, long for long flowers, or short for pecking at the base.

# Back to the burrow

Back in the North Pacific, the tufted puffin had a successful day fishing out in the Bering Sea. Puffins carry whole fish in their bills, holding up to **30 fish** at once. They have backward-pointing spines on the inside of their mouths that keep the fish from falling out while they swim and fly.

Like penguins, puffins have wings that are built for diving and swimming—but unlike penguins, they can also fly! Puffins and penguins aren't closely related to one another, so the fact that they have similar adaptations is called **convergent evolution**.

At the burrow, the puffin chick peeps for food. The parent puts the meal down on the ground for it to eat, one fish at a time. Sometimes the fish are a challenge for the young chick to gulp down!

Puffin wings are difficult to maneuver, so the birds often crash-land into the grass!

A sweet treat

As the day draws to a close, it's time for Cape sugarbirds in South Africa to sneak in a quick meal before bedtime. They feed on nectar from plants, but they also rely on **homemade nectar-feeders** that people put in their yards. The feeders are made from bottles with upward-facing caps, and they are filled with sugary water that resembles nectar.

They are a good feeding alternative for sugarbirds that are struggling to find flowers. Homemade nectar-feeders provide a healthy, ready meal not only for sugarbirds, but also for other nectivores (nectar-eaters) such as malachite sunbirds.

Sugarbirds and sunbirds can also eat **small insects and spiders**, but, like hummingbirds in North and South America, their bills are specially adapted for getting nectar from flowers.

A sugarbird's tail is almost as long as a person's arm!

# Sky dancing

One of the most amazing sights to watch is a giant flock of European starlings in the early evening over cities, towns, and fields. These large gatherings, called **murmurations**, occur at dusk, right before the birds settle in for the night.

Here in Rome, the capital of Italy, the birds start flying one by one, and over time the murmuration grows until it is made up of hundreds and hundreds of birds.

The flock seems to move like a single being, but no individual bird is in charge. The details of how murmurations start, and how the birds don't fly into one another, still baffle scientists! But what causes this elaborate dance in the sky?

Well, it's a way for the starlings to **confuse predators** and keep them from attacking individual birds. Nearby lurks a peregrine falcon. By grouping together, each starling helps protect the others by making a bigger target, so that any one individual is less likely to become dinner for the speedy falcon.

# Bedtime snacks

As night approaches and the sun sets, bugs start to come out. The adult swallows try to get one last meal for their chicks back in the nest. Swallows often **prey on flying insects** like craneflies and horseflies, but when they're lucky they can catch dragonflies or even grasshoppers!

When the adults return to the nest, the chicks cry out and the food is split up between them. So that no chick is left hungry or too full, they have a way to signal how much food they need. A chick's gape, the soft part around the inside of its bill, is brighter if it needs more food and duller if it has already had a meal. This way the parents know exactly who needs an **extra snack** before bed.

**Meanwhile...** Standing out against the dark shrubs and leaves of the rainforests of New Guinea, a Wilson's bird-of-paradise uses its bright feathers to impress a female.

# The silent assassin

With the sun dipping below the horizon, a barn owl is on the hunt. It is on the lookout for small rodents, such as mice and voles. This beautiful owl has broad wings with very fine feathers at the edges that allow it to fly silently and swoop easily between trees and branches. Its unusual face is specially shaped to direct and focus sounds to its ears—the perfect adaptation for life as a predator.

Gliding low over the fields, the barn owl hears a mouse scurrying through the grass. It pinpoints the mouse's location. Against the owl's large talons and **stealth flying**, the mouse doesn't stand a chance. In one fell swoop, dinner is served.

Barn owls are mainly nocturnal, meaning they are most active at night. So even though the sun is about to set, the owl will continue to **hunt through the night**, while most of the world goes to sleep.

The ears of a barn owl aren't in line with each other. This allows the owl to more easily judge where sounds come from.

# Glossary

**Bill**
A bird's beak, which has an upper and a lower part.

**Breeding**
When birds mate, lay eggs, incubate them, and raise their chicks.

**Brood parasitism**
When a bird lays her eggs in the nest of another species.

**Chick**
A young bird, from the time it hatches to the time it fledges (leaves the nest).

**Colony**
A group of birds that breeds and lives together. A colony can be made up of either one species or many.

**Evolution**
How animals adapt to their environment over time and how new species come to exist.

**Flippers**
The wings of a penguin.

**Flock**
A group of birds that flies together.

**Incubation**
The process of keeping eggs warm so the chicks inside can develop.

**Migration**
The journey animals undergo when moving from one ecosystem to another, often in search of food. Most species that migrate will do so twice a year.

**Murmuration**
A large flock of birds, such as starlings, that flies and swirls together to confuse predators.

**Nectar**
The sugary liquid produced by plants—usually in their flowers—to attract pollinators.

**Nests**
Structures where birds lay their eggs. They can build them or use naturally occurring ones, such as holes in trees.

**Nocturnal**
Used to describe an animal that is mostly active at nighttime.

**Scavengers**
Species that eat animals that are already dead.

**Predators**
Animal species that eat other animals (their prey).

**Prey**
Animal species that are eaten by other animals (their predators).

**Talons**
The claws on a bird's feet.

**Torpor**
A deep sleep where an animal's body temperature drops and its heart rate slows down.

# Index

This has been a

# NEON  SQUID

production

*For Finn, Morgan, Kate, Jenn, Tony, Matt, Josh, Max, Jay, and Martin—and anyone else who shares their love of birds and the natural world.*

**Author:** Dr. Alex Bond
**Illustrator:** Henry Rancourt

**Editorial Assistant:** Malu Rocha
**US Editor:** Allison Singer Kushnir
**Proofreader:** Georgina Coles

Created for St. Martin's Press
by Neon Squid
The Stables, 4 Crinan Street,
London, N1 9XW

EU representative: Macmillan
Publishers Ireland Ltd,
1st Floor, The Liffey Trust Centre,
117–126 Sheriff Street Upper,
Dublin 1, D01 YC43

10 9 8 7 6 5 4 3 2 1

Library of Congress Cataloging-in-Publication Data is available.

Printed and Bound by
Leo Paper Products Ltd. in China.

ISBN: 978-1-684-49285-5

Published in March 2023.

www.neonsquidbooks.com